When You Embrace All of You- You Are an Unstoppable Force.

Embody that Energy

LAISSEZ FAIRE

mind • body • spirit

daily wellness

Mon	Tue	Wed	Thu	Fri	Sat	Sun

Meditation

Today's Intention

Moon Phase & Sign

Daily Routine

Movement

Sleep

Hydration Tracker

gratitude

daily tasks

<table>
<tr><td>Schedule</td><td>Healthy Meals</td></tr>
</table>

Schedule

Healthy Meals

- Breakfast
- Lunch
- Dinner
- Snacks

Sleep Rating

①	②	③
Poor	Okay	Well Rested

Ideas for outdoor time

habit tracker

Activity	Mon	Wed	Tue	Thu	Fri	Sat	Sun

Top Things To-Do

Motivational Quote

"

Affirmation of the Week

reflections

doodle

daily wellness

Mon	Tue	Wed	Thu	Fri	Sat	Sun

Meditation

Moon Phase & Sign

Daily Routine

Today's Intention

Movement

Sleep

Hydration Tracker

gratitude

daily tasks

Schedule

Healthy Meals

- Breakfast

- Lunch

- Dinner

- Snacks

Sleep Rating

Poor   Okay   Well Rested

Ideas for outdoor time

habit tracker

Activity	Mon	Wed	Tue	Thu	Fri	Sat	Sun

Top Things To-Do

-
-
-
-
-
-
-
-
-

Motivational Quote

"

Affirmation of the Week

reflections

doodle

daily wellness

Mon	Tue	Wed	Thu	Fri	Sat	Sun

Meditation

Today's Intention

Moon Phase & Sign

Daily Routine

Movement

Sleep

Hydration Tracker

gratitude

daily tasks

Schedule

Healthy Meals

- Breakfast
- Lunch
- Dinner
- Snacks

Sleep Rating

Poor   Okay   Well Rested

Ideas for outdoor time

habit tracker

Activity	Mon	Wed	Tue	Thu	Fri	Sat	Sun

Top Things To-Do

-
-
-
-
-
-

Motivational Quote

"

Affirmation of the Week

reflections

doodle

daily wellness

Mon	Tue	Wed	Thu	Fri	Sat	Sun

Meditation

Today's Intention

Moon Phase & Sign

Daily Routine

-
-
-
-
-

Movement

Sleep

Hydration Tracker

gratitude

daily tasks

Schedule

Healthy Meals

- Breakfast
- Lunch
- Dinner
- Snacks

Sleep Rating

Poor   Okay   Well Rested

Ideas for outdoor time

habit tracker

Activity	Mon	Wed	Tue	Thu	Fri	Sat	Sun

Top Things To-Do

Motivational Quote

"

Affirmation of the Week

reflections

doodle

daily wellness

Mon	Tue	Wed	Thu	Fri	Sat	Sun

Meditation

Today's Intention

Moon Phase & Sign

Daily Routine

-
-
-
-
-
-

Movement

Sleep

Hydration Tracker

gratitude

daily tasks

Schedule

Healthy Meals

- Breakfast

- Lunch

- Dinner

- Snacks

Sleep Rating

Poor   Okay   Well Rested

Ideas for outdoor time

habit tracker

Activity	Mon	Wed	Tue	Thu	Fri	Sat	Sun

Top Things To-Do

Motivational Quote

Affirmation of the Week

reflections

doodle

daily wellness

Mon	Tue	Wed	Thu	Fri	Sat	Sun

Meditation

Moon Phase & Sign

Daily Routine

Today's Intention

Movement

Sleep

Hydration Tracker

gratitude

daily tasks

Schedule

Healthy Meals

- Breakfast

- Lunch

- Dinner

- Snacks

Sleep Rating

Poor   Okay   Well Rested

Ideas for outdoor time

habit tracker

Activity	Mon	Wed	Tue	Thu	Fri	Sat	Sun

Top Things To-Do

Motivational Quote

Affirmation of the Week

reflections

doodle

daily wellness

Mon	Tue	Wed	Thu	Fri	Sat	Sun

Meditation

Today's Intention

Moon Phase & Sign

Daily Routine

Movement

Sleep

Hydration Tracker

gratitude

daily tasks

Schedule

Healthy Meals

- Breakfast
- Lunch
- Dinner
- Snacks

Sleep Rating

1 — Poor
2 — Okay
3 — Well Rested

Ideas for outdoor time

habit tracker

Activity	Mon	Wed	Tue	Thu	Fri	Sat	Sun

Top Things To-Do

-
-
-
-
-
-
-
-

Motivational Quote

"

Affirmation of the Week

reflections

doodle

daily wellness

Mon	Tue	Wed	Thu	Fri	Sat	Sun

Meditation

Today's Intention

Moon Phase & Sign

Daily Routine

Movement

Sleep

Hydration Tracker

gratitude

daily tasks

Schedule

Healthy Meals

- Breakfast
- Lunch
- Dinner
- Snacks

Sleep Rating

Poor   Okay   Well Rested

Ideas for outdoor time

habit tracker

Activity	Mon	Wed	Tue	Thu	Fri	Sat	Sun

Top Things To-Do

-
-
-
-
-
-
-

Motivational Quote

"

Affirmation of the Week

reflections

doodle

daily wellness

Mon	Tue	Wed	Thu	Fri	Sat	Sun

Meditation

Today's Intention

Moon Phase & Sign

Daily Routine

-
-
-
-
-
-

Movement

Sleep

Hydration Tracker

gratitude

daily tasks

Schedule

Healthy Meals

- Breakfast

- Lunch

- Dinner

- Snacks

Sleep Rating

1 — Poor

2 — Okay

3 — Well Rested

Ideas for outdoor time

habit tracker

Activity	Mon	Wed	Tue	Thu	Fri	Sat	Sun

Top Things To-Do

Motivational Quote

"

Affirmation of the Week

doodle

daily wellness

Mon	Tue	Wed	Thu	Fri	Sat	Sun

Meditation

Today's Intention

Moon Phase & Sign

Daily Routine

Movement

Sleep

Hydration Tracker

gratitude

daily tasks

Schedule

Healthy Meals

- Breakfast
- Lunch
- Dinner
- Snacks

Sleep Rating

1 — Poor

2 — Okay

3 — Well Rested

Ideas for outdoor time

habit tracker

Activity	Mon	Wed	Tue	Thu	Fri	Sat	Sun

Top Things To-Do

-
-
-
-
-
-
-

Motivational Quote

"

Affirmation of the Week

reflections

doodle

daily wellness

| Mon | Tue | Wed | Thu | Fri | Sat | Sun |

Meditation

Today's Intention

Moon Phase & Sign

Daily Routine

Movement

Sleep

Hydration Tracker

reflections

doodle

daily wellness

Mon	Tue	Wed	Thu	Fri	Sat	Sun

Meditation

Today's Intention

Moon Phase & Sign

Daily Routine

-
-
-
-
-
-

Movement

Sleep

Hydration Tracker

reflections

doodle

daily wellness

Mon	Tue	Wed	Thu	Fri	Sat	Sun

Meditation

Today's Intention

Moon Phase & Sign

Daily Routine

Movement

Sleep

Hydration Tracker

reflections

doodle

daily wellness

Mon	Tue	Wed	Thu	Fri	Sat	Sun

Meditation

Moon Phase & Sign

Daily Routine

Sleep

Today's Intention

Movement

Hydration Tracker

reflections

doodle

Enjoy!

 Fall Equinox, Mabon, the Harvest. Whatever name you give it, it is a season of balance, where light and dark are equal. We can benefit from embracing this season and resetting our mind, body & spirit.

I hope this journal helps you refocus your attention on habits that will support you and your energy. Use this time to Harvest & be thankful for the seeds you have planted and their growth.

May You Always Grow....

Marquex Faulkner